"UNDER THE BOUGHS" • Ellicottville

"LAST SUN" • Lake Ontario, Chimney Bluffs State Park

Western New York

Wild

Celebrating Our Rich Natural Heritage

'Wild'
Wishes!

DLR

Photography and Text by
David Lawrence Reade

"This book is dedicated to all who support my art. Because of you I am able to continue to share this work that I love, this expression of my heart and soul, this calling that I am every day inspired by and always surprised by."

—David Lawrence Reade

My heartfelt thanks to the following advisors, editors and proofreaders who selflessly contributed to help make this book the best it could possibly be:

Donna Felger, David Maynard, Kristie Maynard, Brian Meyer, David Muller, Barbara Reade, Lawrence Reade, Mike Reade, Adrian Zannin

♦Photography, Text, Layout and Design by David Lawrence Reade♦

For more information about David Lawrence Reade's books, fine art photographic prints or publishing services or to contact him, visit:

www.DLRimagery.com

ISBN: 978-1-879201-58-3

Co-published by:
David Lawrence Reade/DLR Imagery
www.DLRimagery.com
&
Western New York Wares
P.O. Box 733, Ellicott Station
Buffalo, New York 14205
(716) 832-6088
www.buffalobooks.com

Distributed by:
Western New York Wares

Printed in Western New York by:
Dual Printing, Inc.
340 Nagel Drive
Cheektowaga, New York 14225
(716) 684-3825

Disclaimer: Outdoor activities are by their very nature potentially hazardous. All participants in such activities must assume the responsibility for their own actions and safety. The author and publishers of this book assume no responsibility or liability for actions or occurrences should you decide to visit any of the places featured in the 'Wild Guide' or mentioned or pictured anywhere else throughout this book. Do not trespass on private property. Respect closures and barriers of any kind on public land, they are there for your safety and for the protection of wildlife and our natural resources.

Contents

EWORD   6
Why We Love It Here   6
About the Author   7
Natural History and Geography   8

TUMN SPLENDOR   10
Treescapes   12
The Leaves   18

E WONDER OF WATER   22
Lakes   24
Streams & Creeks   30
Waterfalls   36

EST FRIENDS   40
Warm-Blooded   42
Cold-Blooded   48
Fine-Feathered   50
Found on the Farm   54
Web Art   56

D GARDENS   60
Spring   62
Summer   67
Fall   69

N IN NATURE   74
Art in Nature   76
Just Passing Through   80

EST FOR THE TREES   84
The Forest   86
The Trees   92

TER WHITE   96
ce & Lace   98
Winter Woods   104

D GUIDE–FAVORITE ESCAPES   108

Why We Love It Here

Why *do* we love it here—why do more than two million people choose to call this region home? I have posed this question to hundreds of people at art shows. In no particular order, here are their most common answers: four beautiful seasons; the Great Lakes; abundant forests/lack of suburban sprawl/rural charm; less congestion, pollution and traffic; plentiful wildlife; creeks, streams and waterfalls; and finally, interesting topography—hills, foothills and ridges. In short, most mentioned one aspect or another of the *nature* of Western New York.

In pursuit of the next great image I've been to some pretty spectacular places, including Alaska, Hawaii and the Canadian Rockies to name a few. The beauty in these places is almost beyond belief yet, I always return here, to unsung Western New York. Why? Because I know a secret: this area belies tired, old myths; it is a region that abounds with natural beauty just waiting to be explored and enjoyed. Having grown up here, I have spent my life traipsing around these parts and, during the last 20 years, collecting images while I'm at it. I have been lucky enough to have witnessed some truly magical and wondrous scenes. As one who knows these parts pretty well, I can say with no doubt, there is a lifetime worth of real quality natural scenery here. No, it's not at all like Alaska or Hawaii with their obvious beauties. It's a scenic wealth of a closer, more personal and intimate variety, one you can actually live in and not have to be wealthy to enjoy.

Let me tell you a story. I was hiking the day after Christmas in one of my all-time favorite places in Western New York, a deep, spectacular gorge south of Buffalo called Zoar Valley. I chose a lesser known trail in a remote area never expecting that I would see anyone else that day. Nevertheless, as I hiked in, I heard voices. Sure enough, I came upon three people, two brothers and one of their wives enjoying one of the plentiful scenic overlooks. We exchanged greetings and I moved on.

A little further down the trail I stopped to photograph some intriguing ice formations and they caught up with me. They told me that all three of them were originally from this area but that the couple now lived in Fort Collins, Colorado. They went on to say how they loved Zoar Valley and hike it every time they're here. "Geez", I said, "With all that spectacular mountain beauty back in Colorado, you still want to see Zoar Valley again?" The husband-brother said, "With so many nature lovers flocking to the mountains in places like Fort Collins, the trails are often filled with people, whereas here, it feels like wilderness, a place where one can enjoy real solitude." And then he added that "The Rockies are really just high desert, there is nothing nearly so lush and green as here." I had never really thought about either of those points; I had just taken the greenery and serenity for granted.

So what do I hope to accomplish with this book? To celebrate the wonderful wild and natural aspects of this beautiful region by sharing with you over 130 of my very best images; images that I have not only been lucky enough to capture but to experience as well. I present these to you along with a few personal tales from my adventures over the years in the area and some interesting facts about the region that you may not already know. With this book I am attempting to give Western New York its proper due, the place I call home!

The *Wild Guide*

Western New York contains a treasure trove of spectacular parks and natural places to experience. The ***Wild Guide*** (page 108) highlights some of my favorites, a few of which have depth not usually found outside of the Adirondacks. Allegany State Park, for example, contains 65,000 acres of wild, natural beauty. The guide provides a basic description of each locale along with personal insights and 'must see' features. On the first page of each chapter in this book you will find ***Wild Guide*** reference numbers, suggesting which of these places might be best for enjoying that particular chapter's subject.

About the Author

David is a lifelong resident of Western New York who has pursued photography and writing as his full time career since escaping the corporate world in 1996. He has published two previous books about the area, most recently the first of its kind *The Four Seasons of Letchworth—A Celebration of the Grand Canyon of the East* (available from his website and area bookstores). David also photographed and authored the best-seller *Beyond Buffalo, A Photographic Guide to the Secret Natural Wonders of Our Region.*

His images and writing have been used in numerous publications and he has won many awards for his photography. David exhibits and sells his hand-printed photography at fine art shows and from his website: **www.DLRimagery.com**

From the Author/Photographer:

About the Images

I am an intuitive photographer as opposed to a methodical one; I don't scout out locations or plan images in advance. Instead, I let the images call me—my intuition has led me on many a great adventure!

My images will always live on in me as a result of their having evoked powerful emotions at the time I captured them. While all are inspirational, some are cause to reflect on the mysteries and wonder of life itself, while others give me a feeling of profound peacefulness. Some even conjure up a sense of déjà vu, of having been there before.

All my photographs are personally hand-printed by me, in limited editions using the traditional method: in the darkroom from my original negative. No computers, no digital enhancements, what you see is what I saw, plain and simple. The images used in this book were selected from thousands that I have taken in the region over the past 20 years. Each image was carefully scanned and adjusted only for exposure balance and color accuracy, as would be done in the darkroom. These images faithfully represent what I saw through the lens. Thank you picking up this book. I hope you will share in my enjoyment of 'Wild' Western New York!

Mailing List/Images of the Month

For those interested in keeping up with my latest work, I post new images on my website on a monthly basis. To be notified each month when they are available and/or to be notified about upcoming events and special offers, join my mailing list (detailed information is available on the website.)

Natural History and Geography

Geologically speaking, a lot has happened here in Western New York. To sum it up, seas filled and spilled, land folded and eroded, glaciers grew and withdrew and plants and animals resided and died. All of this activity laid the foundation for Western New York today, but it didn't begin to resemble the land we know now until the end of the last period of glaciation about 12,000 years ago.

At that time, the entire region from Canada down to just north of present day Allegany State Park was covered with a massive sheet of ice, the Wisconsin glacier, up to one or two miles thick. The atmosphere warmed and it began to melt. When this great glacier retreated, the predecessors to the Great Lakes were formed and deep gorges (e.g. Niagara, Genesee, Zoar Valley) were scoured by the meltwaters. Moraine deposits (rock and soil that had been scooped up by the glaciers when they were advancing) called drumlins, sometimes quite significant in size, were left behind. (For a great example of a large drumlin, drive Route 436 between Dansville and Nunda - it's quite an impressive hill!) Today, Western New York has three distinct regions—the lake plains to the north, the eroded hills south of the plains and the Allegheny Mountains in the southern area which were untouched by the glacier.

Northern Western New York, comprised of Niagara, northern Erie, Orleans, Monroe, Wayne, Genesee and northern Livingston counties is largely composed of ancient lake plains and is relatively flat or gently rolling except where there are escarpments—erosion-resistant high ridges which once formed the shorelines of ancient lakes. There are two prominent escarpments running through this area, the Niagara and the Onondaga. Anywhere a river or stream topples over the brink of these escarpments, beautiful waterfalls can be found, including the well known Niagara and Genesee High Falls, and a multitude of smaller falls. The elevations here range from about 250 feet at the Lake Ontario shoreline to 800 or 900 feet in the southernmost part.

To the south of Buffalo and Rochester and the lake plains, the elevation gradually increases into the Allegheny Plateau. This region includes Wyoming, Ontario, southern Erie and Livingston counties, and northern Chautauqua, Cattaraugus and Allegany counties. The elevations top out at about 2,000 feet at the summits of the highest hills. When the glaciers retreated, the plateau was eroded into hills bisected by steep valleys, gorges and ravines where streams continue that process today.

Beyond the reach of glaciers in southern Chautauqua, Cattaraugus and Allegany counties and into northern Pennsylvania are found the Allegheny Mountains which reach up to 2,500 feet in places. Allegany State Park in this region escaped glaciation and is the most northerly region of unglaciated landscapes in eastern North America. From the unglaciated summits south of Olean to the floodplain of Cattaraugus Creek northwest of Gowanda, total relief in Cattaraugus County is 1,825 feet, a range of elevation greater than in any other New York county west of the Catskill and Adirondack Mountains.

Western New York must have been a dark and foreboding place for the first European settlers. The tall, dark forests of hemlock, white pine, maple and beech stretched endlessly. Precious little sunlight broke through to the forest floor. The woods were inhabited by predators rarely seen today or completely eradicated, like mountain lions, wolves, bobcats and bears. Where there weren't forests, there were swamps. Great plagues were attributed to these swamps, sometimes killing most of a settlement as it swept through the town. These sicknesses, somewhat like malaria, were known as "Genesee Fever" or "ague"—and many a settler succumbed to them.

Western New York's ancient woods were sheared in the early to mid 1800s. Home sites were carved out of the deep forests. Fields were cleared for farming. Roads were hacked through the dense woods. In a relatively short period of time, most of the ancient forests were 'harvested', transforming the hydrology of the region. When the great forests blanketed this area they acted like a giant sponge resulting in a consistent year-round flow in the creeks and streams that the settlers were able to count on for the milling of grains and timber. When the forests were gone, the creeks and streams became more sporadic—often just trickles throughout the summer, but raging torrents subject to flooding during spring melt and after substantial rains. Today, some of the forests have grown back and although these relatively young forests lack the really deep duff of their ancient predecessors, the flood and drought cycle has been somewhat alleviated.

The cutting of the great forests, draining of the swamps and aggressive hunting changed the wild plant and animal populations as well. Since the top predators have been all but eliminated, deer and turkey are the most often seen larger animals. We have become the top-of-the-food chain predator. Rattlesnakes, common in the area then, are now extremely rare. The plant community once consisted mainly of mature forests and marshland/bog complexes. Today, marshes are rare, most having been drained and old-growth forest is even rarer, only a few thousand acres remain in the entire Western New York region.

Old growth forest, untouched for 150 years or more, has a unique biological ecosystem. Plants have the opportunity to mature (tiny club mosses for example, which only grow in older forests, take 17 years just to reach maturity). The understory is populated with unique (and sometimes rare) plants that are specially suited to the conditions and are typically found nowhere else. One common characteristic of many of these plants is their ability to survive with limited sunlight. And with different plants, different animals also thrive, like the stunning pileated woodpecker that depends on dead and dying trees to house the carpenter ants they eat. These ancient forests and swamps have been replaced by cities and towns, farmland, young new forests and meadows.

Western New York Defined

For the purposes of this book, I consider Western New York to be a broad region, not necessarily defined by lines on a map. For that reason I am including the northern most portion of the Allegheny National Forest in Warren and McKean Counties of northwestern Pennsylvania as well the following New York counties: Niagara, Erie, Orleans, Monroe, Wayne, Ontario, Genesee, Livingston, Wyoming, Chautauqua, Cattaraugus and Allegany. Why include part of Pennsylvania? Because I often explore both Allegany State Park and the National Forest together when I'm in that area and do not differentiate between them just because there is an arbitrary line on a map that runs through it—they are both part of the same beautiful and unique ecosystem.

Autumn Splendor

"Autumn, the year's last, loveliest smile."
—William Cullen Bryant

"Autumn is a second spring where every leaf is a flower."
—Albert Camus

The annual turning of the leaves, alas, always seems to be over too quickly. Here in Western New York we are treated to a grand display of colors—reds, purples, golds, yellows, oranges and all shades in between. In this rich, temperate forest-growing environment, the full range of trees provides all possible shades and hues—our autumn truly goes out in a blaze of glory. Ask someone who lives here what they like best about Western New York and I'd bet that the fall colors are high on the list.

The yellows and oranges we see in the leaves have been there all summer. When the trees stop manufacturing green chlorophyll, preparing to shut down their food making processes for the winter, the green slowly fades away, revealing the brilliant yellows and oranges. In contrast, the bright reds and purples we see in the maples are made mostly in the fall. Glucose, a sugar that plants use for food and as a building block for growing, is trapped in the leaves. Sunlight, combined with cool nights, turns the glucose into brilliant red. The browns of oak leaves are made from wastes left in the leaves. It is this unique combination of all the types of trees here in Western New York and each one's unique color-making mechanism that gives us such a beautiful Autumn display. The splendor is as good as—nay, better than—you will find almost anywhere.

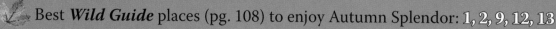 Best *Wild Guide* places (pg. 108) to enjoy Autumn Splendor: **1, 2, 9, 12, 13**

"OUTREACH" • Archery Field Overlook, Letchworth State Park

Above: "GHOST OF A MIST" • Allegheny Reservoir
Page 10: "EYES TO THE SKY" • Boston
Page 11: "FEUILLES COLORÉES" • Ellicottville

"CHROMA-THERAPY" • Red House Lake, Allegany State Park

"POND REFLECTIONS" • Collins

"BLAZE OF GLORY" • Ashford Hollow

"RURAL RUSTIC" • Boston

"AUTUMN'S PALETTE" • East Otto

"THE RED AND THE GREEN" • East Otto

"RESTING PLACE" • Middle Falls area, Letchworth State Park

"TREASURE IN THE SHALLOWS" • Zoar Valley Gorge, Collins/Persia

"FROSTING" • Concord

"MAPLE CASCADE" • Ellicottville

"RIPPLES" • Zoar Valley Gorge, Collins/Persia

The Wonder of Water

"I came where the river — Ran over stones;
My ears knew — An early joy.
All the waters — Of all the streams
Sang in my veins — That summer day."
—Theodore Roethke

Stephen Johnson, EPA Administrator, said while dedicating a new water desalinization plant in Texas: "Water is the lifeblood of our bodies, our economy, our nation and our well being." By that definition, we are wealthy beyond our wildest dreams here in Western New York. We have two of the largest fresh water lakes in the world to our north and east, and a multitude of rivers, streams and creeks crossing the land elsewhere. Freshwater like this can only be dreamed of in many places in the world. It has been said that the next battleground after oil will be related to water and that the struggle to protect and control this precious, life-giving resource may be even more intense.

With our hilly topography and two major escarpments crossing the region, we also enjoy a wealth of scenic waterfalls. The most famous, Niagara, is only one of many in Western New York ranging from dainty little drop-offs in shallow ravines to some up to 500 feet high (seasonally) in Letchworth State Park. I have never seen a waterfall I didn't like no matter how big or how small. There is just something magic about how calm, flowing water gathers force and energy as it spills over the brink, splashes to the bottom, then returns to its calm self like it went crazy for a minute that mesmerizes me. I can sit by a waterfall for hours.

 Best *Wild Guide* places (pg. 108) to appreciate the Wonder of Water: **1, 4, 5, 9, 11, 13**

"SHADES OF SHADOW" • Quaker Lake, Allegany State Park

Above: "GOLDEN DUSK" • Lake Erie, Evangola State Park
Page 22: "MORNING CALM" • Zoar Valley Gorge, Collins
Page 23: "SHORELINE SERENITY" • Quaker Lake, Allegany State Park

"PASSAGE TO AUTUMN" • Red House Lake, Allegany State Park

"CASTLES OF MORAINE" • Lake Ontario, Chimney Bluffs State Park

"BEHIND THE BLUFFS" • Lake Ontario, Chimney Bluffs State Park

"CLOUDLAND" • Quaker Lake, Allegany State Park

The Amazing life of Hellhole Pond

I find myself in a hotel in the middle of an industrial zone, an area that has been sacrificed to the great god of progress. Surrounded by industrial companies and office parks, I feel isolated from nature. As is *my* nature, I have awakened early; I have a couple of hours to kill. So I do what I do, I explore. I walk the roads feeding the industrial parks. I find some green—some hope locked in between the buildings. A tangle of electric lines runs overhead and where they run, there are no buildings. I follow where they lead me. I find mud, muck, dirty marshes and, lo, what's this?—a tiny pond with a couple of old, but functional birdhouses on time-tilted posts along the perimeter hidden from sight at the far edge of an unkempt little three hole golf course.

How long has it been since an "explorer" like me has stumbled upon this forlorn pond I wonder? Amazingly, despite the location, the pond teems with life! In the presence of powerful electromagnetic fields, amid a highway with industrial dirt, dust, and turmoil, surrounded with shredded fast food wrappers flapping in the bushes like prayer flags, still, there are plenty of survivors here. As I stroll the pond's edge, big fat bullfrogs dive into the murky depths. Little birds are in the heat of battle over who gets to reside in the birdhouses. Robins are hopping on the grass, looking? Listening? for worms. Water bugs skim across the pond bottom. I spy miniature dragon flies (damsel flies?) hovering over the surface. There certainly is no lack of life here at what I dub "Hellhole Pond."

I return to my little oasis the next morning. The walk here was tortured by hissing tires, loud motorcycles, grinding gears—the rush hour crowd, with coffee in one hand, cell phone in the other, all five minutes late and trying to make it up—just like yesterday, and the day before, and the day before that.

Two Canada geese couples and their fluffy broods greet me upon arrival. Each couple has three goslings, one group obviously older than the other. The smaller ones are about the size of my fist; the larger about double that. They all stay a wary distance away, moving when I move, grazing when I stop, the parents' eyes always on me. The goslings waddle back and forth like little fuzzy tennis balls with legs, always keeping to momma's flanks. I try to move slowly and smoothly so as not to upset them too much.

I wander the edge of the pond looking for the bullfrogs. Splash! There's one. He makes a run for it. He is huge, actually bigger (or at least longer) than the smallest goslings. The little birds must have settled their apartment dispute since yesterday, for all is quiet around the birdhouses. In the distance, the golfers on the golf course are oblivious of me and this little pond with its teeming life, intent only on whacking a little white ball into a distant little hole.

Finally, it's time to return to the hotel to get ready for my day. I leave with mixed emotions—here is an amazing display of the resilience of life yet I am saddened by the fact that all the pond residents must live amid the clutter, clatter and clamor beneath sizzling power lines. I tell myself they don't know any different. I walk back next to a corridor of green containing a little stream at the edge of the golf course. I spy something white through the bushes down at creek's edge. I push through the scratchy shrubs, slide down the muddy bank and retrieve a gleaming white golf ball half submerged in the mud. I wash it off and take it with me—my good luck charm for the day.

As earlier, I walk along the highway with whizzing cars and trucks just feet from me, but I no longer hear them—the sweet memory of the amazing life at Hellhole Pond insulates me for now. Sometimes it's life's little discoveries like stumbling upon this unlikely sanctuary that make all the difference. My only regret? I have no pictures to share—I didn't have my camera with me!

A Cool Dip

The water was almost bathtub warm on this blazing-hot mid-August day, so "cool" here really means "fun." I was in a funk when my good friend Mike called and suggested we go to Zoar Valley Gorge for the day to get away from it all. I had to agree this would probably be a good thing for me, both mentally and physically, and far better than sitting in a sweltering house, sweating and sulking.

The main and south branches of Cattaraugus Creek feature about twelve miles of stunning gorge, adorned with towering cliffs up to 400 feet high, knife-edge ridges, numerous cascading waterfalls and lush forest. With all that spectacular scenery, just the thought of going to Zoar Valley puts me in a good mood; I love the place. It's been a treat, retreat and refuge for me since I first visited it many years ago. It's my favorite place to celebrate the beauty of nature and to escape from life when times are tough. I've visited the gorge literally hundreds of times and in all seasons. I like to call it "Western New York's Last Wilderness" and, indeed, there are portions of it that have never been logged and truly feel wild, while it's limited accessibility allows real solitude.

We arrived at the Valentine Flats parking area, organized our provisions, then began the hot hike down to the water. It's a gradual descent through the forest, the last portion being an almost tropical tangle of old forest and huge, hanging vines. In summer, this area really does have the look and feel of a jungle. After about 20 minutes of dodging deer flies and swatting mosquitoes, we emerged from the forest to the spectacular panoramic view of high cliffs, deep blue sky and the sweet melody of flowing water.

The water called out to us. We waded in, found a good-sized natural pool (an area where the water has worn a smooth depression in the rock), sat down and immersed our bodies, with only heads and necks exposed letting the rushing water carry away our troubles. Paradise found. The rest of the world faded away, taking my stress with it. And, although the water was warm, it was still refreshing compared to the mid-90 degree air temperature.

"WHITEWATER" • Zoar Valley Gorge, Otto/Persia

After a while, Mike got the itch to body surf in the nearby rapids. We had to keep our feet in front of us to avoid bodily harm, as there were many rocks to dodge. Eventually we located a smooth, deep and clear channel and were able to let the current take us for a considerable distance without worry. Pure bliss! We surfed the channel numerous times, then went back to spend the rest of the afternoon in the pool, just chatting about life in general and relaxing.

Alas, days like these must always come to an end. Daylight was beginning to fade and we were getting hungry, so we reluctantly left the water to begin the trek back to our vehicle. Before leaving, we turned and admired the glowing twilight cliffs as I declared that there is no better way to spend a day than the way we just had and that we must get back here to do this again before the summer is over. Mike agreed, of course. But with our busy schedules we never did make it back again that summer. There's always next year!

"ADRIAN'S PARADISE" • Boston

Spring Melt

Like a moth to a flame, I am drawn to the tiny streams of spring, those little ravines that trickle at most, but more often are dry the rest of the year. They now rush as rivulets coursing with energy, bobbing and bubbling, muttering and murmuring, splashing and spilling on their merry way to join larger creeks and streams downhill.

It's 63 degrees on March 3rd, not a record temperature for this particular day, but close, and the streams have come alive. Predictably, each spring when the temperatures finally rise significantly above the freezing mark, the liquid that has been held captive as snow and ice all winter finds freedom. Today marked the day the fun began. There is something about this throbbing energy after a long, cold winter that causes me to feel as if the water were coursing through *my* veins. I think my blood runs in sympathy with the newly-freed water. I get excited, perhaps partly in anticipation of the longer, warmer, sunnier days to come, and the new growth that will soon be sprouting everywhere from the earth.

So, when the temperature rises well above freezing on a spring day and you can't find me, chances are I'll be deep in the woods somewhere, admiring these little waterways that get only a few chances a year to celebrate their very existence.

"OUT OF THE MIST" • West Valley

"HEADWATERS" • Boston

"LES CHUTES EN COULEUR"—This image is also the front cover of my book:
"The Four Seasons of Letchworth—A Celebration of the Grand Canyon of the East"

"MIDSUMMERS DREAM" • Persia/Otto

"SECRET CASCADE" • Zoar Valley, Collins

"GLEN FALLS" • Glen Park, Williamsville

"BRIDGE OVER TUMBLING WATERS" • Leroy

"HALF FROZEN" • Deer Lick Nature Preserve, Persia

"CASCADE DE SATIN" • Middle Falls, Letchworth State Park

"VIEW FROM ABOVE" • Eden

Forest Friends

The Visitor

Out of the corner of my eye — Something stirs.
Who's here? Who's with me — Deep among the Firs?
A critter, a creature — Whose 'here' is 'home'.
I am but a visitor —A guest where I roam.
–David Lawrence Reade

I like to think of many of the images in this section as 'gifts' I have received over the years. When I set out with camera in tow, I am never specifically searching for wildlife. I am decidedly *not* a 'wildlife photographer'—one who sits and waits in the same spot for hours—I am much too active for that. But being in the woods often has its benefits—occasionally I get lucky when a wild encounter results in some of the images you'll see on the following pages. The animals usually seem more curious about me than afraid and, as long as I don't make any quick movements, are content to stop and gaze back at this weird two-legged creature with a hunk of metal in his hands.

Some may call me sentimental when it comes to wildlife—I'm OK with that, I am quite fond of the animals I share this planet with. For me, it's always a thrill to come across these denizens of the wild, whether it's the heart-pounding explosion of a grouse from the bush, a white-tailed deer rump bounding gracefully off into the distance or a hawk or turkey vulture gliding silently on the thermals far above. Whether or not I squeeze the shutter, I always feel privileged to have crossed paths with my beautiful forest friends.

 Best *Wild Guide* places (pg. 108) for encounters with our Forest Friends: 1, 3, 8, 12

Fawn Rescue

For two straight days it poured. I had cabin fever—I'd been pacing the house like a caged cat. When the tempest finally subsided the next morning, I called a friend and we headed off to hike in the magnificent Zoar Valley Gorge.

With the first sun in two days warming our backs, we carefully picked our way to the bottom of the canyon. There, shafts of sun danced off the crashing waves of a river still pulsing with terrifying energy fueled by runoff from the torrents of the last forty-eight hours. Determined to explore anyway, we threaded our way upstream along the shallows at the edge, careful to avoid the hungry currents. After about an hour, we rounded a bend and there she was—a soaking wet fawn lying, legs akimbo, among the rocks looking equally exhausted and frightened. With our senses overcome by the incessant roar of the churning water echoing off the towering cliffs, we could hardly believe our eyes. She had apparently gotten caught in the floodwaters and been carried helplessly downstream until she was finally able to struggle out to the relative safety of this stony spit of land.

Because a young fawn cannot yet run with the swiftness and assurance that will be its heritage, its only defense is to lie perfectly still. For this reason, it is usually better to leave a lying fawn alone, for the mother is ordinarily just out of sight nearby. In this case however, with this narrow tongue of land completely isolated by raging water and cliffs, there was nowhere for her mother to be hiding. She was probably somewhere far upstream or had been carried away by the raging waters—it was clear the fawn would die without our help. This meant scaling steep bluffs with a precious two-week-old cargo in our arms. At first, the fawn was terrified, but soon she began to relax. By the time we reached the top, she was licking the sweat off our necks (for the salt it contains) and had stopped struggling. My friend took the fawn to a wildlife rehabilitator where she was raised and then released back to where she belongs, leaping through forest and field…

Above: "FOREST ENCOUNTER"
Page 40: "THE ORIGINAL FOREST CITIZEN"
Page 41: "WIZARD" • Barred Owl

"SNOW NOSE"

"FAWN RESCUE"

"TWINS" • Baby Skunks

"NOW WHAT?" • Groundhog

"PEEKABOO" • Red Fox Pup

"OVER... OR UNDER?" • Red Fox Pup

The Fox and the Easter Bunny

It's late afternoon on a warm Easter Sunday and it's been a long but successful work day. Since early morning I've been laying out stone paths behind my house and now I'm whipped. I plop myself down in a chair with a glass of wine and stare unfocused into the woods. That's when "he" trots confidently by. He's small, sleek and beautiful wearing a magnificent reddish coat accented by black-tipped ears, a white underbelly and a fluffy white-tipped tail. "He" (or she for all I know) is a red fox and seems to know exactly where he is going.

He climbs up a narrow, steep ridge and freezes at the top, standing at alert attention. His ears twitch and turn as he observes the valley below. Is he looking for prey? His mate? His pups? I pull out my binoculars for a closer look. As I peer at him, he seems to sense my gaze and turns looking directly into the business end of my binoculars. There is no trace of fear at all in his eyes. After a couple of minutes, he relaxes a bit and sits down. Still ever alert, he swings his head to and fro with his little ears pirouetting like antennae listening for... what? Then it dawns on me—he's looking for the Easter bunny of course! Well, I do suppose any old rabbit will do, as long as he gets a meal. This gets me thinking about a curious question—what does a bunny have to do with the Christian Easter celebration?

Well, as it turns out, nothing really. It seems that the Christians "borrowed" both the name and the symbol from ancient fertility lore. The "Easter hare" was no ordinary animal, but a sacred companion of the old goddess of spring, Eostre. The hare and the rabbit were the most fertile animals known and they served as symbols of new life. Long before the time of Christ, parents told their children that the magic hare would bring them presents at the spring festival. These presents were often painted eggs representing the new life beginning at this time of year.

The fox seems very relaxed now, his constant vigilance on the wane. He lays down and licks and preens himself like a cat. Suddenly, he leaps to his feet and takes off like a shot into the valley below. I can't help but wonder if he is fresh on the trail of a bunny, tracking down his Easter feast...

A Squirrel Will Do Anything...

...to get into a bird feeder. I don't have to tell that to those of you who feed the birds. But I really thought I had the ultimate solution. It consists of a feeder high on a pole, away from any trees or branches, protected with a piece of stovepipe dangling just below the feeder. The stovepipe is free-hanging so if the squirrel tries to jump on it, it swings and he cannot get a grip. And if he tries to climb up the pole inside of it, he reaches a dead-end—it is closed off at the top.

This particular winter a lot of snow fell shortening the distance from the ground to the feeder. With a two foot advantage, the little rascals were able to make the leap around the stovepipe and pull themselves up into the feeder. So, in my abundant wisdom, I dug a wide trench in the snow around the pole so that the distance was again too great for a successful leap. But... I left the shovel standing upright in the snow about six feet away. Wouldn't you know it—a wily squirrel climbed to the top of the handle and flung himself madly towards the feeder—just missing it.

Of course I could have gone out to move the shovel, but this looked like good entertainment and I had to admire his savvy and determination, so I left it standing where it was. Climb, leap, miss. Climb, leap, miss. Climb, leap–made it! Holding on with one sticky little hand, he was able to pull himself up and into the feeder. Amazing! Respecting his tenacity, I let him gorge for a few minutes on well earned birdseed, then scared him off and moved the shovel. You truly have to admire these plucky little creatures!

"SHOULDA GONE SOUTH" • Red Squirrel

"NOW YOU SEE ME..." • Gray Squirrel

The Squirrel and the Tree

As I strolled through the woods one pleasant summer day, I spied a black squirrel leaping through the underbrush, seemingly just enjoying its own agility. I have always had great admiration for squirrels. Their intelligence, nimbleness and persistence never fail to impress me as I watch them connive to empty my bird feeders (see story opposite page). Black squirrels in particular have always fascinated me, probably because they aren't nearly as common as the gray variety.

As I watched this handsome, agile animal leap about, I became aware of a great tree looming nearby that I hadn't noticed before. There, from among a thousand skinny saplings rose a magnificent beech tree. Judging from its size, huge crown and furrowed bark, I guessed that this tree must be at least 200 years old, probably much older. I would imagine that it was quite impressive even 50 years ago, why loggers bypassed it then I don't know. As I considered the quandary of what the loggers might have been thinking in not cutting it, out of the corner of my eye I saw a black streak dash across the forest floor, leap up onto the massive trunk and shoot straight up to the top of the tree. He stopped on a branch high up in the crown of this majestic specimen and peered back down at me. I swear I saw a smug smile flash fleetingly across his little face, as if proud to show off his endearing squirrelly talents to someone.

"DON'T COME ANY CLOSER..." • Garter Snake

"I WARNED YOU..."

"SNEAK ATTACK" • Frog & Red Eft

"LOOK INTO MY EYES" • Barred Owl

"FLEDGLING" • Green Heron

"STANDING HIS GROUND" • Barn Owl

...And Then They Decided to Join Me

From time to time it seems wild animals have decided to join me in my activities. There was the time I was riding my mountain bike down a back country dirt road and when I rounded a corner I almost ran into a flock of wild turkeys. They all scattered in different directions except one—he flew next to me at the same speed I was going at the elevation of my head for a good minute. What a thrill, having this wild bird flying beside me!

Another time I was mowing my lawn, minding my own business, when a grouse jumped from out of the woods and began following me around the yard. Wherever I went, there she was, right behind me. When I turned off the engine, she disappeared in a flash. When I started the engine up again, she was back. "What's going on?" I thought. "Is she angry that I'm making so much noise in the quiet woods?" (I wouldn't blame her for that.) It turns out that my lawnmower engine sounds enough like the drumming mating call of a male grouse that this lovesick bird thought she'd found true love.

The topper though has to be when I was working one warm summer day on an essay titled "Memorial Wilderness," a treatise on how, when it comes to wilderness preservation, we don't set aside enough land for natural ecosystems to function properly. It was mid-afternoon and I was working in my creative room with a pair of screen doors open to the delicate fragrance of the forest wafting in. Except for a few twittering birds and a gentle breeze, all was quiet.

First I sat and got my ideas together. Then I picked up a pen and was about to start writing when, at that very moment, a whole legion of owls began hooting enthusiastically in the woods! In the middle of the afternoon on a beautiful, summer day! When trying to make sense of this, it hit me at some basic level that I had somehow connected with the owls, that they understood and agreed with the conclusions I had drawn and were communicating that to me. It may seem silly to think that this is possible, but what other conclusion could I draw? What else would cause the normally nocturnal owls, during the middle of the day, to gather together in a large group and vocalize with such vehemence? Was it only a wild coincidence? I'll let you draw your own conclusions...

"DO YOU HEAR WHAT I HEAR?" • Wild Turkeys

David Lawrence Reade **51**

Of (Tit) Mice and Men* (and Other Brave Little Birds)

With the advent of spring and the first string of really nice days, I got the itch to do some landscaping. My yard is important to me—I look out onto it from what I call my 'creative' room—where I write, scheme and otherwise hatch ingenious plans that'll make me millions so I can retire and do... what? Well, what I do now of course!

I decided to work on constructing stone pathways that I had been planning for some time but somehow had never gotten around to. Until now. This work involves digging, leveling, hauling and re-leveling until it's gotten right. In other words, lots of movement, sound and a few choice words being muttered from time to time. No bird would dare visit the birdfeeder in the midst of this fray, right? At first none do. Then I am startled by the rapid pulse of little birdwings, 'flpppppp, flpppppp, flpppppp', shooting past my ears. I look up and there they are—a pair of titmice perched on the feeder happily crunching away on sunflower seeds, seemingly oblivious of me and my work.

These adventurous t'mice must have signaled that all was okay, and soon chickadees, juncos and other brave little birds joined them flying amazingly close past my head to the feeder from nearby trees. It made me feel like I was in the middle of a miniature O'Hare Airport during rush hour, with myriad little birds landing, taking off and hanging out in flight patterns waiting for a slot to open at the feeder. And there's no flight controller. I guess one's not necessary; they seem to know the pecking order.

Interesting to me is the fact that no larger birds join the celebration. It seems the bigger the bird, the more skittish they are. I work in bliss with my little friends flapping and twittering around me and somehow this makes my labor seem less arduous. Once that first pair of titmice got up the courage to ignore my presence and the clamor, they all did!

* with apologies to John Steinbeck

"CHRISTMAS CARDINAL"

"LOUD 'N PROUD" • Blue Jay

"SPREADING THEIR WINGS" • Turkey Vultures

"FLEDGLING"

"WATCHFUL EYE" • Mourning Dove

"BOVINE STANCE"

"IS IT SAFE TO COME OUT YET?"

"OUTSTANDING IN HER FIELD"

"SLEEPY EYES"

Part of Western New York's rural charm is seeing our farm friends out in their fields.

"LIKE MOTHER, LIKE DAUGHTER"

"BACKLIT BEAUTY"

"DEWCATCHER"

"DOUBLE FANTASY"

David Lawrence Reade 57

"SILKEN ELEGANCE"

Wild Gardens

"For myself I hold no preferences among flowers, so long as they are wild, free, spontaneous.
Bricks to all greenhouses! Black thumb and cutworm to the potted plant!"
–Edward Abbey

"To analyze the charms of flowers is like dissecting music; it is one of those
things which it is far better to enjoy, than to attempt to fully understand."
–Henry T. Tuckerman

Agreeing with both men, though nowhere near as radical as Abbey, I think that there is nothing more splendid to behold than an exuberant field of wild flowers. Not planted, fertilized, cultivated or modified, these flowers are, as Abbey so succinctly puts it: "wild, free, spontaneous." In the wild, each season spring through fall, brings a whole new regime of flora to enjoy. A few of my personal favorites in our area are trilliums, New England purple asters and dame's rocket. But I love 'em all.

Of course, non-flowering plants are to be appreciated as well. Despite the fact that we are the sunniest and driest area in all of the Northeast from May to September (as close to a perfect summer as you can get, not too hot and lots of sun, even those who flee the winters agree that summers here are wonderful), we usually get just enough rainfall to keep all plant life lush and luxuriant all summer long. Among the non-flowering plants, ferns and their fascinating fiddleheads are at the top of my favorites list—Western New York is positively rich in all types of ferns, from the elegant and small, to the six foot tall.

Note - I have tried my best to identify some of the plants and flowers in this section but I am no expert!

 Best *Wild Guide* places (pg. 108) to admire nature's Wild Gardens: **1, 3, 7, 13**

"SPRING BLISS" • Cherry Tree, Forest Lawn Cemetery

Above: "PATCH O' PLENTY" • Trilliums
Page 60: "PILLARS OF PURPLE" • Bugle/Ajuga
Page 61: "APPROACHING BEAUTY" • Rough-fruited Cinquefoil

"GARDEN OF DELIGHT" • Trillium and Barren Strawberry

"COUNTRY BOUQUET" • Wild Apple

"RHODOS & ROCKS" • Wild Rhododendrons

"SURVIVOR" • Trillium at the base of a much abused beech tree

"FENLAND FINERY" • Dame's Rocket

Fascinating Fiddleheads

'Fiddlehead' is a funny word. It makes me silly when I hear it. Stick another word at the end of 'fiddle' and it always sounds comical. Go ahead, say "fiddlehead." Now "fiddlesticks." Smiling yet? Maybe this is why nonsensical 'fiddle' words are part and parcel of our language, words like fiddle-faddle, fiddle-footed, fiddlebit and fiddle bucket. Often, upon hearing a 'fiddle' word, I burst into song: "fiddle-dee-dee, fiddle dee-dee, the fly has married the bumble bee." Silly me.

But my fascination with fiddleheads runs deeper than the silly sound of the word—they are just so interesting to see, looking like alien periscopes emerging from the earth to take a look around. So what exactly are fiddleheads? They are the unfurled fronds of a young fern. A fiddlehead resembles the curled ornamentation (called a scroll) on the end of a stringed instrument, such as, well, a fiddle or violin. But alien they're definitely not; there are some 75 types of ferns in the northeast United States. But without a doubt, the kings of them all are the Ostrich and Cinnamon ferns. These impressive plants can grow as tall as six feet thereby earning their crown. Their fiddleheads are equally impressive, rising proudly from swampy areas like so many elongated violin necks and sometimes reaching three feet tall before they begin unfurling. Fossil records indicate that ferns have been around for at least 400 million years and once reached heights as high as 150 feet. How I'd love to see the fiddleheads from those giants!

"ALIEN PERISCOPES" • Fiddleheads

Ostrich and Cinnamon ferns grow best in rich soil with constant moisture, often near streams or ponds. They form hard clumps at their base, rising up like platforms from the soggy soil. I am lucky to have a beautiful patch of Cinnamon ferns in a sheltered, low-lying area on my property. I watch eagerly each spring for the first tips to poke up from their bases and from then on it is my pleasure to observe them unfurl throughout the spring until they stand as tall as me. I feel something primitive when I commune with my fern friends, similar to the powerful aura I feel in an old growth forest.

The fertile spore-bearing fronds of the cinnamon fern are erect and shorter than the sterile fronds and become cinnamon-colored, hence the name. The fertile leaves appear first; their green color slowly becomes brown as the season progresses. The spore-bearing stems persist after the sterile fronds are killed by frost, until the next season. The spores must develop within a few weeks or fail.

Ostrich and Cinnamon fiddleheads are sometimes harvested as food in the Northeast. The New Brunswick village of Tide Head bills itself as the Fiddlehead Capital of the World. In the U.S., fiddleheads are sometimes served with cider vinegar and butter in the spring or pickled with dill seed for eating year round. Many people eat them in salads after boiling or steaming. Warning—fiddleheads must be thoroughly cooked—there are toxins in the plant that break down and become harmless only after being subjected to a prolonged period of heat. There have been numerous instances of food poisoning associated with eating raw or lightly cooked fiddleheads.

Both ferns are often used as ornamental plants in gardens. They spread quickly and make excellent ground cover in wet, low-lying areas. These ferns provide seasonal cover and hiding places for ground-frequenting birds such as ovenbirds, water thrushes, wood thrushes, robins and Carolina wrens. They also serve as protection for frogs and toads. Fern folklore: Fern "seeds" are said to render one invisible if gathered on Midsummer's Eve (on or around the summer solstice). Ferns are also said to be an herb of immortality.

Fiddleheads provide me with pleasure in three ways: the humorous name; observation of the fascinating unfolding; and the final product—lush and elegant fern gardens. Who could ask for more from a plant that grows naturally all around us?

"FINE FILICALE" • Bracken Fern

"CINNAMON STICKS" • Cinnamon Fern

"SUNLOVER" • Wild Sunflower

"STREAMSIDE SURPRISE" • Tiger Lily

"FALL PROFUSION" • Goldenrod, New England Purple Aster, Purple Coneflower (Echinachea)

"MORNING AT WATER'S EDGE"

"HANGING GARDEN"

"AT YOUR FEET"

"ASTRAL ELEGANCE" • New England Purple Aster

Man in Nature

Edward Abbey said: "...the itch for naming things is almost as bad as the itch for possessing things" and he is right on both counts in my opinion. But we will continue to do both as it seems to be in our nature. Many of the names we use every day and take for granted had rich meaning to the Native Americans. Ontario means "beautiful or pleasant lake." Canandaigua, the birthplace of the Seneca Nation, means "the chosen spot or place." Conesus meant "sheep berries." Honeoye signifies "finger-lying," referring to its shape. Irondequoit Bay was aptly named meaning "where the lake turns aside." Sodus Bay has been translated to mean "silver waters."

Names Upon the Land

Ye say they all have passed away, That noble race and brave,
That their light canoes have vanished, From off the crested wave;
That 'mid the forest where they roamed, There rings no hunter's shout;
But their name is on your waters, Ye may not wash it out."
- Lydia Huntley Sigourney

Genesee is "the pleasant valley." Niagara was named meaning "the neck," apparently referring to the Niagara Peninsula. Tonawanda means "swift water." The village of Nunda was named because that is "where the hills come together." Canawaugus and Cattaraugus have roughly the same meaning "foul-smelling water" or "foul-smelling banks" because of the natural gas that seeped through from the shale. Gowanda was appropriately named as "below the cliffs." The town of Cheektowaga is "the land of the crabapple." Lake Erie and the county of Erie were named after the Erie tribe which, roughly translated, means "the cat people." Chautauqua Lake was appropriately named as the place "where the fish were taken out."

 Best *Wild Guide* places (pg. 108) to experience Man in concert with Nature: 6, 7, 9

Above: "CASTLE TOWER" • Griffis Sculpture Park, East Otto
Page 74: "NATURE RECLAIMS" • East Otto
Page 75: "REFLECTIONS OF THE PAST" • Ashford Hollow

The Bishop marries the King (Art) and Queen (Nature) symbolizing the wedding of art and nature in this very special place.

"ROYAL WEDDING" • Griffis Sculpture Park, Ashford Hollow

"THE BATHERS" • Griffis Sculpture Park, East Otto

David Lawrence Reade   77

"FLAT MAN 'N THE MOON" • Griffis Sculpture Park, Ashford Hollow

"THE DANCING LADY" • Griffis Sculpture Park, Ashford Hollow

"PLACIDITY" • Red House Lake, Allegany State Park

"SUNSET CRUISE" • Lake Erie

"PADDLE YOUR OWN CANOE" • Red House Lake, Allegany State Park

"BRIDGE TO A VIEW" • Rim Trail, Letchworth State Park

"FALL FANTASIA" • Rimrock, Allegheny National Forest

"LIGHTER THAN AIR" • Letchworth State Park

Forest for the Trees

"The clearest way into the universe is through a forest wilderness."
–John Muir

"In the woods, too, a man casts off his years, as the snake his slough, and at what period soever of life is always a child."
–Ralph Waldo Emerson

According to the great naturalist Henry David Thoreau, "sauntering" is the art of taking walks. The word comes to us from the middle ages, when idle people went to "Sainte Terre," or the Holy Land. Thus, a saunterer was a seeker of holy lands. To me, the forests are the holy lands and a walk in the woods is a sacred event. A saunter rarely fails to refresh my spirit—and fortunately, we have plenty of forest here in Western New York in which to do so.

Around most cities in this great land, farmland is being sold off and the forests are being stripped for what has now become known as suburban sprawl. It's happening here too, but at a slower pace, which is good for those of us who consider the forest our temple. I maintain that nature is the best educator of all—observe it, strive to understand it, and you will learn all you really need to know.

When I was a child, there was nothing I liked better than to go 'sploring.' My whole world was outdoors; when I wasn't playing sports, I was in the woods. Entering the dark forest was always equal parts mystery and excitement, for I never knew what I'd discover there. Today, I still feel that same mix of eager anticipation and reverence for those mysteries. And when life is tough, it's a healing place where the rest of the world and my troubles disappear and I become that excited child again.

 Best *Wild Guide* places (pg. 108) to see the Forest for the Trees: 1, 2, 10, 12, 13

"ESCAPE TO THE WOODS" • Letchworth State Park

Above: "ENCHANTED FOREST" • Rimrock, Allegheny National Forest
Page 84: "CANYON CANOPY" • Zoar Valley Gorge, Gowanda/Collins
Page 85: "MUSCLE BEECH" • Concord

"CANYON SUNRISE" • Letchworth State Park

"ILLUMINATION" • Letchworth State Park

Shadow Lands

Early morning, *very* early morning, that all too brief time of shadowy light and awakenings, is easily my favorite time of the day. It is a time when all seems possible and yesterday's disappointments and problems but distant memories. It's as if I'm awake but part of me is still in dreamland. From the first dim glow to just after the sun has cleared the horizon is a time like no other. Here in dawn's bosom I am renewed, at the pinnacle of my sensitivity and creativity. The currency of my best creativity is usually spent by noon, with the remainder of the day then devoted to the necessary, mundane and routine.

Naturally, I love to be outdoors at dawn, preferably in a forest or a desert or the mountains well away from the civilized world. Steve McQueen said "I'd rather wake up in the middle of nowhere than in any city on earth." My sentiments exactly. The air in these special places is often so still I feel like the earth is holding its breath, waiting to exhale until after the sun comes up. As I glide through the morning ozone I can feel its velvety smoothness, its palpable weight, I feel like a swimmer gliding through water but without getting wet.

Dawn colors are deep and rich, not yet bleached by the blast of full sun. Sometimes there are mists, those beautiful curtains of slowly shifting hanging humidity that hide away portions of a scene in an ever-changing collage of endless possibilities where no two visions are ever exactly alike. Mist and fog are to nature what slight of hand is to the magician—now you see it, now you don't. Ah, mystical shadow

"GODLIGHT" • Rimrock, Allegheny National Forest

Rock Cities

It may surprise you to find out that there are 'cities' in our forests! Yes, "rock cities" are scattered throughout the southern tier and into Pennsylvania, by some counts, 30 or more. These fascinating places are formed by the combined effects of erosion and gravity on rocky hilltops, not, as many have surmised, by glaciers leaving these boulders behind. In fact, if the glaciers had reached these "cities," they would have been pulverized out of existence by the undeniable force of those massive sheets of ice.

These rocks are old! They once lay at the bottom of a vast sea that blanketed the area. It is hard to believe that what is now hilltop was once sea bottom. About one-half billion years ago, these curious places were just hills capped with a highly erosion-resistant type of rock called pudding stone. Eventually however, even this rock yielded to the inexorable force of erosion (wind, water, freezing and thawing, plant roots) forming cracks and crevices. Gravity then took over gradually pulling the now separated slabs of rock down the hillsides. These actions continue today although imperceptibly slowly.

Besides the rocks themselves, I find the plant life fascinating in rock cities. Many trees that live on the tops of these monoliths have root systems that extend all the way down the sides to the ground below, appearing like the tentacles of an octopus. And because some areas between boulders receive so very little sunlight, all manner of intriguing mosses, lichens and ferns abound.

When the region was first settled, the larger cities were big tourist attractions. Several are still operated for profit, but the tourist traffic has declined in recent years as more people became familiar with them and realized just how common they were. One such park, appropriately named Rock City, was once a Native American fort and signal station.

There are a number of rock cities to visit located on public land. Among them are Little Rock City in Ellicottville, the Thunder Rocks and the Bear Caves in Allegany State Park and Rimrock and Jakes Rocks in the Allegheny National Forest. If you haven't ever been to one, it's well worth a visit. And if you, like me, have gone many times, find some people who haven't been there and take them along. It's just so much fun watching their faces light up when seeing a rock city for the first time!

"FAERIE LAND" • Rimrock, Allegheny National Forest

"LAND AND THE RISING SUN" • Ashford Hollow

"ALONE AT TWENTY BELOW" • Concord

"BARK ART" • Sycamore Tree

"TENACIOUS" • Zoar Valley Gorge, Gowanda/Collins

"GOLDEN EXHALATIONS OF THE DAWN" • Ellicottville

Winter White

I Heard a Bird Sing

I Heard a bird sing... In the dark of December
A Magical Thing... And sweet to remember
"We are nearer to Spring... Than we were in September."
I Heard a bird sing... In the dark of December
-Oliver Herford

Winter, the season we all love to complain about. Well, not me! I enjoy winter not only as a photographer but as an explorer and casual observer too. This is a time of complete contrasts, an exciting new look that comes only during that season, when we trade in our greens for shining and sparkling whites to contrast with the grays and browns of nature. There's nothing I enjoy more than beholding a fresh blanket of snow upon the woods and meadows. I received an e-mail recently titled "You Have To Be From Buffalo To Get It" that summed it up well: "People who live in areas subject to hurricanes, tornadoes, floods, droughts, forest fires, mudslides and earthquakes can't BELIEVE that we would live in an area that gets this much snow." What? I'll trade a mantle of beautiful snow-white for any of those other horrid things any time.

There is a cure for the short days and gray skies that many complain about. Strap on a pair of cross-country skis or snowshoes and head for the nearest park or woods when opportunity affords. You'll fall in love, as I have, with the shimmering, dazzling snow-whites and the refreshing, invigorating chill air. I've never seen happier, more fun-loving people than the ones I meet on the winter trails!

 Best *Wild Guide* places (pg. 108) in which to surround yourself with Winter White: 1, 3, 9, 10

Above: "GLISSADE" • Zoar Valley Gorge, Gowanda/Collins
Page 96: "FLEETING BEAUTY" • Middle Falls, Letchworth State Park
Page 97: "ICY ISLANDS" • Allegany State Park

"BLUE ICE" • Little Rock City, Great Valley

"WINTER WILLOW" • North Collins

"FROSTY FALLS" • Bridal Falls, Allegany State Park

"FIRST SNOW" • Concord

Lost!

The temperature is four degrees outside and the wind is howling. The wind chill is fifteen or twenty below zero. Time for a hike! "A hike you say? Are you crazy? It's time to sit by the fire and drink hot cocoa or sip some wine." But for me, the conditions are too good (bad?) to stay inside. It's about an hour and a half before sunset when I set out, bundled up against the cold. The ground is covered with about six inches of freshly fallen snow and because of the sudden drop in temperature earlier, the white stuff is frozen to the tree branches and trunks despite the blustery wind. It's breathtakingly beautiful. And breathtakingly cold. But I warm up fast as I trudge and suddenly all these layers seem foolish, just added weight. But I am used to extra weight, carrying up to 30 pounds of camera gear wherever I go.

I follow deer trails whimsically, not paying much attention to where they lead me. I cross several deep ravines and streams and suddenly realize I am in an intriguing new area I haven't explored before. It is beautiful here; I am surrounded by majestic and snow-laden hemlocks and pines reaching for the sky. I dub the area "Cathedral Grove."

Now the intensity of the snow picks up, it is getting late and the light is beginning to wane. I should turn around but I don't want to leave this new-found oasis. I spot a little hunting shack here that hasn't been used in years, crumbling back to the earth becoming once again the source of the materials from which it was constructed. I feel history here. Perhaps good times have been shared by several men (it's almost always men) bunking together in this tiny bungalow, escaping everyday life for a while, enjoying the camaraderie and feeling adventurous. I can understand their feelings except that I do all my hunting with a camera instead of a gun. Wandering some more, I come upon a woodpecker totem. It's a standing tree trunk, long dead, about ten feet tall, with so many holes in it of varying dimensions and depths, it almost looks like it was deliberately carved. I definitely need to remember how I got here so I can see it again sometime.

"BOREAL LIGHT" • Ellicottville

Realizing that it's now getting seriously
dim, I decide I had better head back. The snow pours down
even more heavily now and I can barely see ten feet in front
of me. I'd better follow my tracks back, I think to myself,
but they're rapidly being filled in with snow, both blown and
falling from the sky. It is hard to tell whether a depression is mine
or made by one of my 'deer' friends at this point. I feel the slightest bit
of panic. I haven't brought supplies of any kind—surely you can't get
lost in Western New York. But in the dark without any light source
it's a different world. And it is definitely going to be a bitter night.
As I move forward, I carefully examine each print to make
sure it is mine. It's amazing how similar deer trails and
boot trails can look with enough new snow on them.
I spot a large hollow created by a fallen tree's root
ball and wondered if it is my fate to spend the night
shivering inside it. I cross one, two,
three ravines sniffing out my trail
like a dog but with my eyes to the
ground instead of my nose. Suddenly, I recognize a familiar
group of trees—I am safe! Relief floods over me to know that I
won't be found frozen days later after all in a fetal position looking like
a giant red puffball squeezed in among the roots of a fallen tree.

"THROUGH THE WOODS" • Allegany State Park

David Lawrence Reade **105**

"PURE AS THE DRIVEN SNOW" • Ellicottville

Wild Guide - Favorite Escapes

Provided here are a baker's dozen of my favorite places to go 'into the wild.' Some may already be familiar, but read on... On the first page of each chapter in this book you will find *Wild Guide* reference numbers referring to the numbers assigned here to each location; these suggest the best places to experience the subject of that chapter. The information below is an overview; please consult the websites provided for more details. Enjoy!

1 ALLEGANY STATE PARK

Description: 65,000 mostly wild acres, the largest wilderness on this side of the state. Features lakes, streams, mountain foothills and old-growth forest.

Features/Best For: Autumn, creeks, flora, forests, hiking, lakes, snowshoeing, X-C skiing, wildlife

Why I like it here: Get away from the roads and you will have no trouble finding solitude; loads of hiking trails. Great bushwhacking. Beautiful in all four seasons. Large trees and some old-growth forest. One could visit here dozens of times and still find new places to explore.

Must See: Gorgeous trilliums and fascinating fiddleheads (immature ferns) can be found almost everywhere in spring. In summer, follow a creek deep into the forest through a paradise of moss-covered boulders and beautiful ferns. Hike through old-growth forest and notice how different the plant community is and how big some of the trees are. Admire the construction of a beaver dam and lodge. During the fall, the hill panoramas are simply stunning. In winter, snowshoe off the beaten track into your own private wilderness. Admire the ice-covered spectacle of 75 foot Bridal Falls.

Location: South-central Cattaraugus County; three entrances off Route 17/I-86 near Salamanca.

More Info: www.nysparks.state.ny.us/parks

2 ALLEGHENY NATIONAL FOREST

Description: One half million acres, much of it 'working forest' sacrificed to extractive industries, but a multitude of special spots have been set aside for the nature lover featuring rock cities, old-growth forest and stunning scenic overlooks. The Allegheny reservoir contains over 90 miles of shoreline.

Features/Best For: Autumn, canoeing, forests, hiking, lakes, rivers and streams, rock cities, scenic overlooks

Why I like it here: Someone with foresight identified some real gems and preserved them for us all to enjoy. Many of these sights are generally unknown to the public at large and hence are lightly visited especially during off-seasons and early in the day.

Must See: Rimrock overlook in the fall. Jakes Rocks. Tionesta and Hearts Content Old-Growth Forests.

Location: Mainly in Warren and McKean Counties of PA between the cities of Warren and Bradford. Contact the U.S. Forest Service–Allegheny National Forest for more information and maps.

More Info: www.fs.fed.us/r9/forests/allegheny

3 BEAVER MEADOW AUDUBON CENTER

Description: A 324-acre nature preserve laced with trails and dotted with scenic ponds both large and small.

Features/Best For: Flora, hiking, ponds/wetlands, snowshoeing, X-C skiing, wildlife

Why I like it here: Great wildlife and bird viewing. Eight miles of well maintained trails for casual hiking/snowshoeing/cross-country skiing; a swamp boardwalk great for observing wetland fauna and flora.

Must See: Hike the Beaver Pond trail early in the morning when all is quiet except for the bird activity in full swing. Snowshoe or cross country ski the forest trails on a sunny winter day and you'll joyfully commune with the chickadees, rabbits and deer.

Location: West-central Wyoming County; Welch Rd. off SR-77, North Java

More Info: www.buffaloaudubon.com/centers.htm

4 CHAUTAUQUA GORGE

Description: An impressive steep-walled gorge called by some "The Grand Canyon of Chautauqua."

Features/Best For: Creek, fossils, gorge, hiking, interesting geology, wading

Why I like it here: An escape deep into the earth beneath towering rock walls. Very primitive feeling with fascinating geology throughout.

Must See: Hike beyond the popular areas into what feels like your own private wilderness. Look for interesting rocks and 400 million year-old fossils. In the summer, cool off in the various swimming holes.

Location: Southwestern Chautauqua County; Hannum Rd., Mayville

More Info: www.dec.ny.gov/lands/42257.html

5 CHIMNEY BLUFFS STATE PARK

Description: An undeveloped state park containing a bizarre landscape of spires, pinnacles and knife-edged ridges stretching a full half mile along the Lake Ontario shoreline.

Features/Best For: Hiking, Great Lake shoreline, unique landscape

Why I like it here: Nothing else like it in this area. Beautiful undeveloped Great Lake shoreline. This moonscape is constantly eroding; return a few years later and the formations will all have changed.

Must See: Hike the ridge trail behind the bluffs for a stunning view of the formations from above overlooking Lake Ontario, then return along the beach for a totally different perspective.

Location: Northeastern Wayne County; Garner Rd., Lake Bluff (near Sodus Bay)

More Info: www.nysparks.state.ny.us/parks

6 FOREST LAWN CEMETERY

Description: An enchanting, country-estate-like cemetery with rolling hills, ponds, a meandering creek, lush vegetation and towering trees.

Features/Best For: City nature escape, creek, flora, ponds, walking

Why I like it here: A 269-acre peaceful and quiet refuge from city hustle and bustle. Great for casual strolls admiring the funerary art while communing with nature. As wild as it gets in the middle of a city!

Must See: The flowering trees in the springtime. Serenity Falls. Gorgeous reflections in the pond surfaces on quiet days.

Location: Erie County; City of Buffalo between Main Street, Delavan Avenue, and Delaware Avenue

More Info: www.forest-lawn.com

7 GRIFFIS SCULPTURE PARK

Description: Over 250 magnificent sculptures integrated with 400 acres of rolling hills featuring trails, ponds, forest and wildflowers .

Features/Best For: Awesome art in a natural setting, autumn, flora, forest, hiking, ponds

Why I like it here: The fantastic imagination of Larry Griffis Jr. and other artists comes alive here; the setting couldn't be better. A beautiful melding of art and nature in the hills, meadows and forests—nothing else like it in the area. Superb hiking.

Must See: Try to find as many sculptures as you can! Many are hidden away deep in the woods. Climb the Castle Tower for a great view of the surrounding hills. Walk or drive slowly past the Rohr Hill Rd. section at dawn or dusk for an eerie experience.

Location: North-central Cattaraugus County; two sections: Rohr Hill Rd., Ashford Hollow; Mill Valley Rd., East Otto

More Info: www.griffispark.org

Wild Guide - Favorite Escapes

8 IROQUOIS NATIONAL WILDLIFE REFUGE

Description: Over 10,000 acres of hardwood swamps, fresh water marshes, forests and meadows teeming with waterfowl, birds and wildlife.

Features/Best For: Hiking, ponds/wetlands, wildlife viewing

Why I like it here: Plentiful wildlife, especially in the spring. Over 250 species of birds, 40+ species of mammals, and all manner of reptiles, fish, amphibians and insects have been observed. Bald eagles have nested here.

Must See: With a variety of pulloffs, overlooks, parking lots and trails, one can never predict what wildlife will be seen at any one point. Visit all you can, you're bound to get lucky, especially in the spring. Note: despite the paradoxical name "Wildlife Refuge", hunting is permitted here and access may be restricted at times.

Location: Southwestern Orleans and northwestern Genesee Counties; in the towns of Alabama and Shelby.

More Info: www.fws.gov/northeast/iroquois

9 LETCHWORTH STATE PARK

Description: It is called the "Grand Canyon of the East" with good reason: the seventeen mile long canyon plunges to depths of over 550 feet in places while the Genesee River below cascades over three major waterfalls. A crown jewel of the New York State Parks System.

Features/Best For: Autumn, flora, forests, gorge, hiking, river, overlooks, waterfalls

Why I like it here: Easily accessible beauty, but also an expansive hidden side of the park to explore that will satisfy the adventurer.

Must See: Beyond the obvious: trek the southern portion of the Finger Lakes Trail on the east side of the park for some of the same stunning vistas as the west side but without the crowds; Hike along the Silver Lake Outlet Creek to discover three hidden waterfalls; After a winter cold snap, view the incredible ice formations of frozen Middle Falls (bring binoculars or a telephoto lens!)

Book Available: To see over 100 glorious images of the park in all four seasons, purchase my book "*The Four Seasons of Letchworth—A Celebration of the Grand Canyon of the West*" (Available at all major bookstores or from my website www.DLRimagery.com.)

Location: Southeastern Wyoming and southwestern Livingston Counties; entrances in the towns of Portageville, Castile, Perry and Mount Morris.

More Info: www.nysparks.state.ny.us/parks

10 MENDON PONDS MONROE COUNTY PARK

Description: Unique glacial geology (for which it was designated a National Natural Historic Landmark). 2,500 acres of ponds, meadows and woods of which 550 acres are undeveloped and have been set aside as a nature preserve.

Features/Best For: City nature escape, flora, wild forest, unique geology, hiking, ponds, wildlife, snowshoeing/ X-C skiing

Why I like it here: Only a few minutes from the city of Rochester. Plentiful ponds and marshes provide for good birdwatching. There are two faces to this park—the easily accessible part with trails, sledding hills, canoe access points and buildings and then there is the wild side—a large nature preserve with no roads, buildings or other improvements.

Must See: Explore the unique glacial geology throughout the park—the high trail on the west esker provides great views. Hand-feed the hungry and tame chickadees along the BirdSong trail in the winter (bring your own black oil sunflower seeds!) Great place to cross country ski or snowshoe in the winter, canoe or hike in the other seasons.

Location: South-central Monroe County; town of Mendon—about 10 miles south of the city of Rochester.

More Info: www.monroecounty.gov/parks-mendonponds.php

NIAGARA GORGE STATE PARKS

Description: Seven miles of wild and rugged gorge accompanied by the roaring pulse of the Niagara River.

Features/Best For: City nature escape, flora, unique geology, hiking, major river and gorge

Why I like it here: Despite the city industry and tourism present on both sides of the gorge, it's very wild and scenic within. The raw power of the awesome Niagara River is something to behold and feel. Many interesting rock formations and some rare plants and flowers can be found here too.

Must See: Hike any or all of the gorge trails in Artpark, Devil's Hole and Whirlpool State Parks and you will be amazed. Experience—see, hear and feel—the Whirlpool and the Whirlpool rapids area, where the entire Great Lakes water flow channels through this narrow gorge. Behold the awesome churning and unstoppable force that is the Niagara River.

Location: Western Niagara County; in and just north of the city of Niagara Falls

More Info: www.nysparks.state.ny.us/parks

STATE & COUNTY FORESTS

Description: Tracts of public land abound throughout Western New York, some up to nearly 5,000 acres in size. Because they have not been developed as parks, most of these oases are unfamiliar to the public at large.

Why I like it these forests: So many to choose from, each with its own unique attractions. Even some of the names entice, such as 'Rattlesnake Hill,' 'Bald Mountain,' 'Braddock Bay,' 'Palmers Pond,' and 'Lost Nation.'

Features/Best For/Must See: Varies by location. Some of the highlights include: forests, meadows, ponds, streams, waterfalls, gorges and lake shoreline. Contact the N.Y. State Department of Environmental Conservation (DEC) or local county authorities for more information.

Locations: Throughout Western New York.

More Info: www.dec.ny.gov/34531.html or local county websites

ZOAR VALLEY STATE FOREST

Description: I call this place "Western New York's Last Wilderness". Its miles of spectacular remote wild canyon reaching depths of over 400 feet is highlighted by interesting geology, old growth forests and a multitude of waterfalls feeding Cattaraugus Creek.

Features/Best For: Autumn, creek, flora, forests, gorge, hiking, overlooks, waterfalls, wildlife

Why I like it here: This is my favorite 'wild' place of all in our region. I've visited here hundreds of times, and each time I discover new features. It really does feel wild and remote and there is so much to discover, enjoy and appreciate. In summer, there's no better place to cool off than in the pools of Cattaraugus Creek.

Must See: The towering gorge walls throughout. The confluence of the south and main branches of the creek. The various waterfalls spilling over the gorge rim in spring or after a good rain. Old-growth forest. Spring and summer wildflowers. The breathtaking views from the rim trail in any season.

Location: South-central Erie and northwestern Cattaraugus Counties; access in the towns of Collins and Persia

More Info: www.zoarvalley.org

Disclaimer: Outdoor activities are by their very nature potentially hazardous. All participants in such activities must assume the responsibility for their own actions and safety. The author and publishers of this book assume no responsibility or liability for actions or occurrences should you decide to visit any of the places featured in the 'Wild Guide' or mentioned or pictured anywhere throughout this book. Do not trespass on private property. Respect closures and barriers of any kind on public land, they are there for your safety and for the protection of wildlife and our natural resources.

"AUTUMN VIEW" • Rimrock, Allegheny National Forest